1. **What do we call the puzzle cube that has to be twisted so that the colours match on all sides?**
   a: Rubik's Cube **b:** Ruben's Cube
   c: Roman's Cube **d:** Rotating Cube

2. **Which objects do you need for a game of Yahtzee?**
   a: Tickets **b:** Dice
   c: Counters **d:** Marbles

3. **Bridge is a card game.**
   a: True **b:** False

4. **There are more black squares than white squares on a draughts board.**
   a: True **b:** False

5. **In which game do you search for your opponent's flag?**
   a: Game of the Goose **b:** Chess
   c: Stratego **d:** Ludo

6. **Children used to spin their top by hitting it with a whip.**
   a: True **b:** False

How many pieces are there on a stratego board at the beginning of the game?

08

7. **The name 'Lego' is derived from the Danish words for 'play well'.**
   a: True **b:** False

8. **Which game involves sliding pucks along a wooden table?**
   a: Bowling **b:** Shuffleboard
   c: Bowls **d:** Mikado

9. **What is the centre of a dartboard called?**
   a: Bullseye **b:** Catseye
   c: Centre eye **d:** Tigerseye

10. **Scrabble is a number game.**
    a: True **b:** False

Games

12. What did Thomas Edison invent?
   a: The light bulb
   b: The computer
   c: The radio
   d: The telephone

13. What did people make weapons with during the Stone Age?
   a: Wood and plastic
   b: Gold and silver
   c: Stone and bones
   d: They didn't have weapons back then

14. Another word for a computer screen is a monitor.
   a: True **b:** False

15. The first digital computers were much smaller than today's computers.
   a: True **b:** False

16. Around which year was the first ever flight in an engine-powered aircraft made?
   a: 1700 **b:** 1800 **c:** 1900 **d:** 2000

17. What did Louis Braille invent?
   a: The chair **b:** The question mark
   c: The football **d:** Braille

18. The tin opener was invented before the tin.
   a: True **b:** False

19. How many wheels did the first engine-powered car have?
   a: 2 **b:** 3 **c:** 4 **d:** 5

20. The first TV remote control was wireless.
   a: True **b:** False

21. The word 'telephone' comes from Greek.
   a: True **b:** False

22 *Brain challenge*

What is the fuel that is used to power planes?

Kerosene

Technology and inventions

28. **The oldest musical instrument in the world is:**
a: A guitar **b:** A flute
c: A drum **d:** A triangle

29. **A short film set to music is called a music video.**
a: True **b:** False

30. **All famous singers and musicians can read music.**
a: True **b:** False

23. **What do you call the set of five lines on which music notes are written?**
a: The stave **b:** The steve
c: The stove **d:** The stiff

31. **What is the part of a song called that is repeated at least once?**
a: The couplet **b:** The chorus
c: The ballade **d:** The aria

24. **Which of these 4 instruments is NOT a stringed instrument?**
a: Guitar **b:** Violin
c: Trumpet **d:** Harp

32. **A musical usually comprises:**
a: Just acting **b:** Just singing
c: Just dancing **d:** Acting, singing and dancing

25. **Adolphe Sax invented the saxophone.**
a: True **b:** False

26. **Pianos usually have 10 foot pedals.**
a: True **b:** False

27. **What is a composer?**
a: Another word for singer
b: Someone who plays other people's music
c: Someone who doesn't like music
d: Someone who writes music

Music

33. What is another word for spaceman?
a: Astronomer **b:** Astronaut
c: Autonomous **d:** Astrophysician

34. In what year did man first set foot on the Moon?
a: 1809 **b:** 1969
c: 1989 **d:** 2009

35. Mars is nicknamed the Red Planet.
a: True **b:** False

36. Venus is the smallest planet in our solar system.
a: True **b:** False

37. What is another word for 'shooting star'?
a: Black hole **b:** Falling planet
c: Meteor **d:** Comet

38. What is a space station?
a: A research laboratory in space
b: A petrol station in space
c: Another word for rocket
d: A type of shop for spacemen

43 *Brain challenge*

What were the first words Neil Armstrong spoke when he landed on the Moon?

That's one small step for a man, one giant leap for mankind

39. There has never been a woman in space.
a: True **b:** False

40. Most planets are named after ancient Greek and Roman gods.
a: True **b:** False

41. The first mammal to orbit around the Earth in a spaceship was a cat.
a: True **b:** False

42. How much does an astronaut's spacesuit weigh on Earth?
a: 1 kilo
b: 11 kilos
c: 110 kilos
d: 1,100 kilos

Space

44. Which of Winnie the Pooh's friends bounces on his tail?
a: Piglet **b:** Tigger
c: Eeyore **d:** Christopher Robin

45. In the Three Little Pigs, the third pig makes a house from ...
a: Straw **b:** Wood **c:** Stone **d:** Iron

46. Dracula is a vampire.
a: True **b:** False

47. Where was Superman born?
a: Mars **b:** Krypton **c:** Earth **d:** Venus

48. What colour are the Smurfs?
a: Red **b:** Yellow **c:** Green **d:** Blue

49. Thumbelina was born in a flower.
a: True **b:** False

50. Snoopy is Charlie Brown's dog.
a: True **b:** False

51. What is Spiderman's real name?
a: Clark Kent **b:** Peter Parker
c: Bruce Banner **d:** Tony Stark

52. How many years did Sleeping Beauty sleep for?
a: 10 **b:** 100
c: 1,000 **d:** 1 million

53. The bell-ringer of Notre Dame is also known as Quasimodo.
a: True **b:** False

Fairy tales and fantasy

44: b 45: c 46: a 47: b 48: d 49: a 50: a 51: b 52: b 53: a

59. You can build a sandcastle underwater with ordinary beach sand.
a: True **b:** False

60. When you look at the concave side of a spoon, you see yourself...
a: Exactly the same as always
b: Upside-down
c: In profile
d: From behind

61. Oil dissolves in water.
a: True **b:** False

62. Spacemen have a bigger head when they're in a space station than they do on Earth.
a: True **b:** False

63. What is the boiling point of water in degrees Celsius?
a: 10 **b:** 50 **c:** 100 **d:** 1,000

54. If you were to need braces fitted to your teeth, you would go to...
a: An orthodontist **b:** An iriscopist
c: An paragnost **d:** An archeologist

55. Echo is another word for the reflection of sound off a surface.
a: True **b:** False

56. You are much heavier in space than you are on Earth.
a: True **b:** False

57. What force is responsible for pulling you downwards on Earth?
a: Ground force **b:** Weight force
c: Gravity **d:** Heavity

58. Warm air rises.
a: True **b:** False

Science

64. Your nose, mouth, eyes, ears and skin are known as your sense organs.
a: True **b:** False

65. A newborn baby recognises its mother mainly by her face.
a: True **b:** False

66. What is the coloured part of the eye called?
a: Amber **b:** Iris
c: Luca **d:** Mira

67. Which part of the body is the most sensitive to touch?
a: Your bottom **b:** Your tummy
c: Your knees **d:** Your fingertips

68. You hear because your eardrum picks up vibrations in the air.
a: True **b:** False

Brain challenge

What is a Homo sapiens?

A human.

69. What is the most common eye colour on Earth?
a: Green **b:** Blue
c: Brown **d:** Grey

70. Humans can hear underwater just as well as above water.
a: True **b:** False

71. Which part of the head helps you balance?
a: Your ears **b:** Your nostrils
c: Your cheeks **d:** Your lips

72. What are the black dots in the middle of your eyes called?
a: Papils **b:** Pepils
c: Popils **d:** Pupils

73. Adults can taste more than children.
a: True **b:** False

Biology

Brain challenge

What is the fastest growing plant in the world?

Bamboo

75. What do you call a miniature tree?
a: Bamboo **b:** Bonsai
c: Oak **d:** Mini tree

76. Which textile grows on a plant?
a: Cotton **b:** Silk
c: Wool **d:** Nylon

77. Ripe fruit is usually harder than unripe fruit.
a: True **b:** False

78. Where do badgers live?
a: In the mountains **b:** Underwater
c: In the forest **d:** On grassy plains

79. Rainbows are created when sunlight meets raindrops.
a: True **b:** False

80. What do you hear when you hold a shell to your ear?
a: The sea
b: Your footsteps
c: Your stomach grumbling
d: The blood flowing through your veins

81. All female mammals produce milk for their young.
a: True **b:** False

82. You can see stars better in the city than in the countryside.
a: True **b:** False

83. Some trees can be eaten.
a: True **b:** False

84. Which fruit is usually used to make wine?
a: Bananas **b:** Oranges
c: Grapes **d:** Strawberries

Nature

91. Complete the sequence: 2, 4, 6, 8, ?
a: 9 b: 10
c: 11 d: 12

92. There are 60 seconds in an hour.
a: True b: False

93. An oval has no corners.
a: True b: False

94. Which number doesn't belong here?
a: 15 b: 25
c: 67 d: 75

86. How many sides does a rectangle have?
a: 2 b: 3
c: 4 d: 6

87. 16 + 7 =
a: 19 b: 21
c: 23 d: 25

95. On a dice, which number is on the opposite side to the 6?
a: 1 b: 3
c: 4 d: 5

88. 4+2 is more than 5+3
a: True b: False

89. 18 - 9 = 9
a: True b: False

90. Which is the most?
a: A millilitre
b: A litre
c: A decilitre
d: A centilitre

96 *Brain challenge*

How many angles does a heptagon have?

L

97. **Which is the largest continent on Earth?**
a: Asia **b:** North America
c: Africa **d:** Europe

98. **Which theory explains the movements of the world's surface?**
a: Plate tectonics **b:** Surface theory
c: Kinetics **d:** Volcanism

99. **New York is the capital of the United States of America.**
a: True **b:** False

100. **Deserts are always made up of white sand.**
a: True **b:** False

101. **How long does it take the Earth to turn once on its axis?**
a: 1 hour **b:** 24 hours
c: 1 week **d:** 1 year

102. **What is another name for the world's land masses?**
a: Continues **b:** Cantons
c: Colonnades **d:** Continents

103. **It's around 6,000 degrees Celsius at the centre of the Earth.**
a: True **b:** False

104. **On which continent can Japan be found?**
a: Europe **b:** Africa
c: Asia **d:** South America

105. **Christmas is in winter all across the world.**
a: True **b:** False

106. **It always rains in a rainforest.**
a: True **b:** False

The Earth

Brain challenge

In which year were the first Olympic Games held?

1896

107. What makes up the symbol of the Olympic Games?
a: 3 stars b: 5 rings
c: 7 triangles d: 9 squares

108. The stages in a football match are known as 'sets'.
a: True b: False

109. A baseball team has 9 players.
a: True b: False

110. How many pins are there in a bowling game?
a: 5 b: 10 c: 15 d: 20

111. Another word for table tennis is 'ping-pong'.
a: True b: False

112. A volleyball may only be touched once before going over the net.
a: True b: False

113. Which sports require a goal?
a: Football and hockey
b: Football and tennis
c: Hockey and tennis
d: Tennis and volleyball

114. In which country did ice hockey originate?
a: China b: Egypt
c: Canada d: Brazil

115. The duathlon is a sporting event that comprises two different types of sport.
a: True b: False

116. How long has archery been a sport?
a: Around 100 years
b: Around 1,000 years
c: Around 5,000 years
d: Over 10,000 years

Sport

123. The Eiffel Tower is shorter in winter than in summer.
a: True **b:** False

124. What did the first inhabitants of Australia use boomerangs for?
a: Playing **b:** Chopping wood
c: Digging **d:** Catching birds

125. The most widely spoken language in China is called Mandarin.
a: True **b:** False

118. Which continent does the potato come from?
a: Europe **b:** South America
c: Africa **d:** Asia

126. Historically, Tsar is a word used to refer to a Russian king.
a: True **b:** False

119. What is the Tower of Pisa famed for?
a: Being one of the highest towers
b: Being one of the smallest towers
c: Leaning **d:** Being triangular

127. Which party is Brazil famed for worldwide?
a: Christmas party **b:** Harvest party
c: New Year's party **d:** Carnival

120. Many discoveries made by explorers were accidental.
a: True **b:** False

121. Paper money existed before coins.
a: True **b:** False

122. In which country will you find many pyramids?
a: Canada **b:** South Africa
c: Thailand **d:** Egypt

128 *Brain challenge*

How many states are there in the United States?

50

World travellers

129. The biggest animal on Earth is the blue whale.
a: True **b:** False

130. A lion has a more powerful bite than a crocodile.
a: True **b:** False

131. The most poisonous animal in the world is:
a: A snake **b:** A jellyfish
c: A spider **d:** A frog

132. Which animal can run the fastest?
a: A cheetah **b:** A lion
c: A springbok **d:** A horse

133. The hummingbird is the only bird that can fly backwards.
a: True **b:** False

134. Which mammal was the first non-human astronaut to orbit the Earth in space?
a: An ape **b:** A rabbit
c: A cat **d:** A dog

135. Which animal has got the largest eyes?
a: The giant tortoise **b:** The giant squid
c: The bigeye tuna **d:** The bigeye mackerel

136. Which bird lays the biggest eggs?
a: The eagle **b:** The swan
c: The stork **d:** The ostrich

137. The dolphin can dive the deepest of all marine animals.
a: True **b:** False

138. The mayfly, also known as the dayfly, lives for...
a: A week **b:** A few days
c: A day **d:** A few hours

Amazing animals

Brain challenge

149

How many coloured blocks does a Rubik's Cube have?

26

139. What colour is a billiard table?
a: Yellow b: Purple
c: Orange d: Green

140. Which chess piece is the most powerful?
a: The bishop b: The knight
c: The queen d: The king

141. A boomerang comes back when you throw it.
a: True b: False

142. What is the lowest number card in a standard deck of playing cards?
a: 1 b: 2 c: 3 d: 4

143. Playmobil has been around for 50 years.
a: True b: False

144. Black begins in draughts.
a: True b: False

145. How many railway stations are there in Monopoly?
a: 1 b: 2
c: 4 d: None

146. You can stop overnight at an inn in the Game of the Goose.
a: True b: False

147. Which game has dragons, seasons, flowers and wind directions?
a: Chess b: Boggle
c: Game of the Goose d: Mahjong

148. How many sides does a dice have?
a: 2 b: 4
c: 6 d: 8

139: d 140: c 141: a 142: b 143: b 144: b 145: c 146: a 147: d 148: c

Brain challenge

Who is believed to have invented baseball?

Alexander Cartwright

150. The bagpipes were invented in Scotland.
a: True b: False

151. There was no sound in the first films.
a: True b: False

152. What material was the first computer mouse made from?
a: Plastic b: Wood
c: Iron d: Glass

153. Where was the first mobile call made from in 1946?
a: A church tower b: A swimming pool
c: A car d: A grass field

154. Rudolf Diesel invented the diesel engine.
a: True b: False

155. A pixel is a small coloured dot or square on a screen.
a: True b: False

156. What do we call a portable computer that you can use on your lap?
a: A hard drive b: A top computer
c: A desktop d: A laptop

157. Who is believed to have invented the scissors?
a: Thomas Edison b: Leonardo da Vinci
c: Alexander Bell d: Edward Scissorhands

158. A kilo of iron is heavier than a kilo of feathers.
a: True b: False

159. On the first computers...
a: People could only make presentations
b: People could only make texts
c: People could only do calculations
d: People could only use the internet

Technology and inventions

Brain challenge

How many strings are there on a classical violin?

161. **How many lines are there in a stave?**
a: 4 b: 5 c: 6 d: 7

162. **What kind of instrument is a djembe?**
a: A wind instrument b: A percussion
instrument c: A stringed instrument
d: A keyboard instrument

163. **There are never more than 3 different
instruments in an orchestra.**
a: True b: False

164. **Someone who plays an organ is called an
organist.**
a: True b: False

165. **Which of the following is a wind
instrument?**
a: A xylophone b: A banjo
c: A clarinet d: A gong

166. **What is another name for the leader of an
orchestra?**
a: A choreographer b: A conductor
c: A composer d: A cabaret performer

167. **Cows produce more milk when listening to
loud and lively music.**
a: True b: False

168. **LP is short for long-playing record.**
a: True b: False

169. **What is a plectrum?**
a: A cloth that is used to polish a saxophone
b: A small flat tool that is used to play a
guitar c: Another word for a black key on a
piano d: A drum stick

170. **What is the more common term for
'rhumba shakers'?**
a: Maracas b: Triangles
c: Flutes d: Rattles

Music

172. Planet is from the Greek word for:
a: Wanderer b: Large stone
c: Earth d: Life

173. ISS stands for international space station.
a: True b: False

174. Which event is described by the term 'solar eclipse'?
a: The Moon moving directly between the Earth and the Sun b: The Earth moving directly between the Moon and the Sun c: The Sun moving directly between the Moon and the Earth d: Solar eclipses only exist in fairytales

175. There is a space telescope orbiting the Earth. What is it called?
a: Trubble b: Bubble
c: Hubble d: Wubble

182 Brain challenge

Who was the second man on the Moon?

Edwin 'Buzz' Aldrin

176. The first man in space was in space for less than 2 hours.
a: True b: False

177. Every planet has at least one moon.
a: True b: False

178. Who was the first man in space?
a: Yuri Gagarin b: Neil Armstrong
c: André Kuipers d: Alan Shepard

179. Which planet is the biggest?
a: Mars b: Venus
c: Jupiter d: Saturn

180. Only robots work at a space station.
a: True b: False

181. Human footprints could remain unchanged on the Moon for millions of years.
a: True b: False

Space

183. **Tintin is bald.**
    a: True b: False

184. **Fred Flintstone lives in the Stone Age.**
    a: True b: False

185. **What is the yellow Teletubby called?**
    a: Tinky Winky b: Lala c: Po d: Dipsy

186. **What type of animals are Winnie the Pooh and Baloo?**
    a: Donkeys b: Rabbits
    c: Bears d: Apes

187. **Batman lives in Gotham City.**
    a: True b: False

188. **What do we call the stone that Obelix (from Asterix and Obelix) often carries on his back?**
    a: Prehistoric stone b: Menhir
    c: Tapir d: Lik stone

193 *Brain challenge*

Name three of Santa's reindeer.

Dasher, Dancer,
Prancer, Vixen,
Comet, Cupid,
Donder, Blitzen,
Rudolph.

189. **Shipwrecked, Gulliver awakes to find himself on an island, tied down by giants.**
    a: True b: False

190. **Which dwarf is not one of Snow White's seven dwarfs?**
    a: Doc b: Dopey
    c: Grumpy d: Gimli

191. **What is Pinocchio's father called?**
    a: Jappy b: Gepetto
    c: Gideon d: Stromboli

192. **Rumpelstiltskin could spin diamonds from straw.**
    a: True b: False

Fairy tales and fantasy

194. If you were to swing a bucket of water very fast in a circular motion above your head and back down again, the water would not fall out.
a: True **b:** False

195. It's easier to lift someone up in water than on dry land.
a: True **b:** False

196. Sound is a vibration in the air.
a: True **b:** False

197. Salt water freezes...
a: Faster than water that doesn't contain salt
b: Slower than water that doesn't contain salt
c: Just as fast as water that doesn't contain salt **d:** None of the above; it can't freeze

198. What colour do you get if you mix blue and yellow?
a: Purple **b:** Orange
c: Grey **d:** Green

204 Brain challenge

What is sodium chloride more commonly known as?

Salt

199. A seismologist knows a lot about earthquakes.
a: True **b:** False

200. When can you see a rainbow?
a: When the Sun shines and it's raining
b: When the Sun shines and it's dry
c: When there is rain but no sunshine
d: When there is neither rain nor sunshine

201. What was once rubbed on split lips as a remedy to help them heal?
a: Snot **b:** Earwax
c: Spit **d:** None of the above

202. If you stand on your head, your head will turn red because more blood flows into it.
a: True **b:** False

203. A balloon inflated with normal air rises.
a: True **b:** False

205. Babies can't hear anything before they are born.
a: True **b:** False

206. When your nose is completely blocked...
a: You can taste food better
b: You can't taste food as well
c: Food tastes the same as always
d: Food tastes different, i.e. much more bitter

207. If you look over your right shoulder with your left eye, you will see...
a: Nothing **b:** Everything behind you
c: Your nose **d:** Your back

208. Your pupils get bigger in bright conditions.
a: True **b:** False

209. Our sense of smell is much more sensitive than our sense of taste.
a: True **b:** False

210. Which taste do newborn babies prefer?
a: Sweet **b:** Salt
c: Sour **d:** Bitter

211. When can you hear better?
a: When you hold your hands over your ears
b: When you extend your ears with your hands
c: When you put your fingers in your ears
d: When you hold your hands and fingers near your ears

212. Humans have thinner skin than animals.
a: True **b:** False

213. Which structures form part of the eye?
a: The iris **b:** The retina
c: The cornea **d:** All of the above

214. Babies blink fewer times a minute than adults.
a: True **b:** False

215 *Brain challenge*

Which is the largest artery in the human body?

The aorta

Biology

216. When someone is good at looking after plants and flowers, we say that he or she has...
a: Green eyes **b:** A green heart
c: Green vision **d:** Green fingers

217. Flowers use scent to attract insects.
a: True **b:** False

218. Seaweed doesn't have roots.
a: True **b:** False

219. How should you stand in order to see a rainbow?
a: With your back to the sun and your face to the raindrops
b: With your back to the sun and the raindrops
c: With your face to the sun and your back to the raindrops
d: With your face to the sun and the raindrops

220. Fruit trees produce flowers before they produce fruit.
a: True **b:** False

221. Mushrooms are a type of:
a: Plant **b:** Flower
c: Animal **d:** Fungus

222. What do you call someone who doesn't eat meat?
a: Veganaut **b:** Vegetarian
c: Rechewer **d:** Carnivore

223. A spruce is a pine tree.
a: True **b:** False

224. It rains harder on one side of a mountain than the other.
a: True **b:** False

225. What does a herbologist study?
a: Trees for use in carpentry
b: Plants for medicinal use
c: Herbs for culinary use
d: Flowers for religious rituals

Nature

Brain challenge 236

What is 3 x 16?

8h

226. **A pyramid is the same as a cube.**
   a: True **b:** False

227. **A boat sails 10 kilometres in an hour. In 2 hours it will have sailed 15 kilometres.**
   a: True **b:** False

228. **What shape is a pentagram?**
   a: A circle **b:** A square
   c: A spiral **d:** A star

229. **2 x 7 = 14**
   a: True **b:** False

230. **A restaurant has 10 tables for 2 persons. How many people can eat at the restaurant?**
   a: 10 **b:** 15 **c:** 20 **d:** 25

231. **How many grams are there in a kilo?**
   a: 10 **b:** 100
   c: 1,000 **d:** 10,000

232. **There are 10 millimetres in a centimetre.**
   a: True **b:** False

233. **Which number is missing in the following sequence?**
   3, ?, 9, 12
   a: 4 **b:** 5
   c: 6 **d:** 7

234. **There is an equal number of girls and boys in a class of 26 children. How many girls are in the class?**
   a: 12 **b:** 13
   c: 14 **d:** 15

235. **A trapezium has 5 corners.**
   a: True **b:** False

Mathematics

237. How long has the Earth existed?
a: Around 460 years
b: Around 46,000 years
c: Around 4.6 million years
d: Around 4.6 billion years

238. What shape is Italy on the map?
a: A car **b:** A pizza
c: A boot **d:** A house

239. The water in the Dead Sea is very salty.
a: True **b:** False

240. Precious stones grow on precious stone trees and bushes.
a: True **b:** False

241. Which is the biggest country in the world?
a: Canada **b:** Russia
c: China **d:** Brazil

242. Which of these mountains is the highest?
a: Mont Blanc **b:** Kilimanjaro
c: Table Mountain **d:** Mount Everest

243. Brick is harder than diamond.
a: True **b:** False

244. New Zealand is located in Oceania.
a: True **b:** False

245. What city is also known as 'The Big Apple'?
a: Tokyo
b: Los Angeles
c: New York
d: Rio de Janeiro

246. The South Pole is a desert.
a: True **b:** False

247 *Brain challenge*

Which sea separates Africa and Asia?

The Red Sea

The Earth

248. Polo is ...
a: A type of flying sport
b: Basketball on ice
c: Underwater wrestling
d: Like hockey but on horseback

249. In which sport can you hit a home run?
a: Football **b:** Handball
c: Baseball **d:** Volleyball

250. The rules for football were created over 100 years ago in England.
a: True **b:** False

251. In figure skating, skating as fast as possible is the most important aspect.
a: True **b:** False

252. In which country did table tennis originate?
a: Tanzania **b:** China
c: Turkey **d:** Germany

253. Which sport does not involve the use of a racket?
a: Tennis **b:** Squash
c: Netball **d:** Badminton

254. The title Prima Ballerina refers to the leading female ballet dancer in a ballet company.
a: True **b:** False

255. A hockey match lasts 20 minutes.
a: True **b:** False

256. What is in a football?
a: Feathers **b:** Stones
c: Water **d:** Air

257. Which sport involves galloping?
a: Bicycle racing **b:** Baseball
c: Horse riding **d:** Badminton

Sport

Brain challenge

Which country is meant by Helvetia?

Switzerland

258. People pay with euros in all European countries
a: True b: False

259. The sun doesn't set for weeks in the summer in the tip of Northern Europe
a: True b: False

260. China is where you can find...
a: The Long Wall
b: The Stone Wall
c: The Great Wall
d: The Zigzag Wall

261. Which continent was inhabited by people first?
a: America b: Asia
c: Europe d: Africa

262. Pyramids are made from very light stones.
a: True b: False

263. What is the currency of Japan?
a: Yin b: Yan c: Yen d: Yon

264. Which word is used to describe popular Indian films that feature a lot of music?
a: Bollywood b: Dollywood
c: Indywood d: Wollywood

265. Spanish is the official language of Australia.
a: True b: False

266. What is Antarctica?
a: The collective name of all the oceans
b: The collective name of all land masses
c: The North Pole
d: The South Pole

267. The Earth has three equators.
a: True b: False

World travellers

258: b 259: a 260: c 261: d 262: b 263: c 264: a 265: b 266: d 267: b

269. Which of the following animals has the longest tongue?
a: The giraffe **b:** The anteater
c: The frog **d:** The snake

270. The great white shark can smell a drop of blood from more than a kilometre away.
a: True **b:** False

271. The anteater eats the most ants of all animals. How many does he gobble a day?
a: Three hundred **b:** Three thousand
c: Thirty thousand **d:** Three million

272. The fastest animal in the world is:
a: The cheetah
b: The swordfish
c: The peregrine falcon
d: The cockroach

273. The largest bird is:
a: The giant albatross **b:** The sea eagle
c: The stork **d:** The ostrich

274. Birds lay the most eggs of all animal species.
a: True **b:** False

275. The wood frog survives in the winter by almost completely freezing.
a: True **b:** False

276. Which animal has the longest nose of all animals?
a: The long-nosed monkey
b: The hog-nosed snake
c: The giant anteater
d: The elephant

277. Which is the most common type of animal on Earth?
a: Insects **b:** Birds **c:** Mammals **d:** Reptiles

278. The cockroach is the fastest insect.
a: True **b:** False

279

Brain challenge

How many eyes does a garden spider have?

8

Amazing animals

280. The first Lego bricks were made from wood.
a: True b: False

281. Twister is played on black and white circles.
a: True b: False

282. Which game requires a steady hand?
a: Connect Four b: Cluedo
c: Operation d: The Settlers of Catan

283. In which game do you try to earn as much money as possible?
a: Risk b: Monopoly
c: Twister d: Shuffleboard

284. Risk is not a board game.
a: True b: False

285. Halli Galli is played with a bell.
a: True b: False

286. A standard pack of playing cards comprises both red cards and black cards. The reds are:
a: Hearts and clubs
b: Clubs and spades
c: Spades and diamonds
d: Diamonds and hearts

287. Which piece will you not find on a chess board?
a: A knight b: A pawn
c: A horse d: A bishop

288. The board game Go has been played for over 200 years. Which country is it from?
a: China b: Russia
c: Mexico d: Greece

289. Mikado is played with coloured marbles.
a: True b: False

Games

290. The inventor of the first modern computer was Konrad Zuse.
a: True **b:** False

291. What are films without sound called?
a: Noiseless films **b:** Silent films
c: Image films **d:** Quiet films

292. The first ice lolly was invented by accident, by a child who left his drink outside in the winter.
a: True **b:** False

293. What does the word 'telephone' mean?
a: Tele means 'close' and phone means 'sound' **b:** Tele means 'far' and phone means 'sound' **c:** Tele means 'to talk' and phone means to 'listen' **d:** Tele means 'to talk' and phone means 'tube'

294. Potato chips were invented by accident...
a: When an angry chef wanted to teach a dissatisfied customer a lesson **b:** When a chef wanted to divide his last few potatoes between a large group of guests **c:** When a sous chef accidentally dropped potato peel into a deep fat fryer **d:** When a researcher in a laboratory overcooked some potato slices

295. The keys on all computer keyboards start with the letters QWERTY.
a: True **b:** False

300 Brain challenge

What is 'whirlybird' slang for?

A helicopter

296. Which instrument can be used to examine tiny objects?
a: Binoculars **b:** A stethoscope
c: A microscope **d:** A telescope

297. WWW stands for World Wide Wikipedia.
a: True **b:** False

298. On which part of a computer are photos and music saved?
a: The round drive **b:** The square drive
c: The soft drive **d:** The hard drive

299. What do you call a small program that can be installed on your telephone?
a: An upp **b:** An app
c: A click **d:** An icon

Technology and inventions

301. **Beethoven wrote music while he was deaf.**
a: True b: False

302. **The first flutes were made from reindeer bones.**
a: True b: False

303. **What does a choreographer do?**
a: He creates a film to accompany music
b: He designs a dance to accompany music
c: He writes a book to accompany music
d: He paints a painting to accompany music

304. **Which of the following men was not a composer?**
a: Mozart b: Columbus
c: Beethoven d: Bach

305. **Scotland is famous for the bagpipes.**
a: True b: False

311 **Brain challenge**

What do we call the lowest male singing voice?

Bass

306. **The djembe comes from:**
a: Australia b: South America
c: Africa d: Asia

307. **A xylophone is an instrument with keys you press to make music.**
a: True b: False

308. **What is the next musical note?**
Do - Re - Mi - Fa - So ...
a: Si b: Do c: La d: Re

309. **Which of these instruments is nothing like a piano?**
a: Synthesizer b: Organ
c: Bassoon d: Keyboard

310. **There are no wind instruments in a brass band.**
a: True b: False

Music

312. How many times does the International Space Station orbit the Earth each day?
a: Twice **b:** 4 times **c:** 16 times **d:** 256 times

313. Which Roman god is the planet Neptune named after?
a: The god of war
b: The god of the underworld
c: The god of agriculture
d: The god of the sea

314. Solar eclipses happen much more frequently than lunar eclipses.
a: True **b:** False

315. There is no wind or water on the Moon.
a: True **b:** False

316. Who was the first man on the Moon?
a: Neil Anderson **b:** Neil Armstrong
c: Buzz Aldrin **d:** Buzz Lightyear

317. The Sun is a:
a: Planet **b:** Planetoid
c: Star **d:** Comet

318. The planet Mercury is closest to the Sun.
a: True **b:** False

319. Saturn has spectacular rings around it.
a: True **b:** False

320. How long does it take sunlight to travel from the Sun to Earth?
a: Slightly longer than 8 seconds
b: Slightly longer than 8 minutes
c: Slightly longer than 8 hours
d: Slightly longer than 8 days

321. In space, noises are...
a: Louder than on earth
b: Softer than on earth
c: Just as loud as on earth
d: Inaudible

Space

Brain challenge

What are Cinderella's stepsisters called?

Anastasia and Drizella

322. The immensely rich uncle of Huey, Dewey and Louie is called Donald Fortune.
a: True b: False

323. A sphinx has the head of a human and the body of an animal.
a: True b: False

324. Who loses her glass slipper?
a: Sleeping Beauty b: Snow White
c: Tinker Bell d: Cinderella

325. What is Lucky Luke's horse called?
a: Black Beauty b: Jolly Jumper
c: Phar Lap d: Lightning

326. Nemo is a clownfish.
a: True b: False

327. What is Obelix's dog called?
a: Dogmatix b: Bobby c: Pluto d: Lassie

328. Which vegetable gives Popeye strength?
a: Beans b: Broccoli c: Spinach d: Potatoes

329. Who becomes green and strong when he is angry?
a: The Bulk b: The Balk
c: The Halk d: The Hulk

330. SpongeBob's best friend is a seahorse.
a: True b: False

331. What is Winnie the Pooh's favourite treat?
a: Jam b: Ice cream
c: Honey d: Blueberries

Fairy tales and fantasy

333. **What conclusion did Isaac Newton arrive at when he saw an apple fall from a tree?**
a: That only ripe apples fall from trees
b: That apples fall faster than feathers
c: That the Moon will also fall on the Earth
d: That gravity exists

334. **Thunder always follows lightning during a storm.**
a: True **b:** False

335. **Which two colours do you mix to get purple?**
a: Red and orange **b:** Red and blue
c: Blue and yellow **d:** Blue and green

336. **What is a light year?**
a: The first half of a century
b: The distance that light travels in a year
c: A year with lots of sunshine
d: The time that a planet takes to orbit the Sun

337. **You can sometimes see circular rainbows from a plane.**
a: True **b:** False

343

Brain challenge

How many arms does a snowflake always have?

9

338. **The Beaufort scale is used to measure wind intensity.**
a: True **b:** False

339. **What is meant by fauna?**
a: The entire world **b:** The human world
c: The animal world **d:** The planet world

340. **A magnet...**
a: Attracts silver **b:** Attracts gold
c: Attracts stone **d:** Attracts iron

341. **The higher you climb up a mountain, the warmer it gets.**
a: True **b:** False

342. **Light bulbs produce both light and heat.**
a: True **b:** False

Science

344. Fair skin protects you better from the Sun than dark skin.
a: True b: False

345. Boys' nails grow slightly faster than girls'.
a: True b: False

346. Where is the smallest bone in the body found?
a: Your nose b: Your ear
c: Your toe d: Your shoulder

347. The strongest bone in your body is...
a: Your lower leg b: Your lower arm
c: Your lower jaw d: A bone in your lower back

348. Every day you lose small amounts of the top layer of your skin.
a: True b: False

349. Adults have more bones than newborn babies.
a: True b: False

350. Roughly how many bones are there in your body?
a: 2 b: 25 c: 650 d: 10,000

351. There are three bones in your forefinger. What are they called?
a: Balanges b: Lalanges
c: Malanges d: Phalanges

352. The heart of an adult beats faster than that of a child.
a: True b: False

353. Who has more hair on their head (on average)?
a: People with dark hair
b: People with blond hair
c: People with red hair
d: Everyone has the same amount of hair

Biology

344: b 345: a 346: b 347: c 348: a 349: b 350: c 351: d 352: b 353: b

354. In a tropical rainforest, it's...
   a: Cold and humid
   b: Cold and dry
   c: Warm and humid
   d: Warm and dry

355. A cloud is a large collection of tiny water droplets in the air.
   a: True **b:** False

356. A flash of lightning warms the air.
   a: True **b:** False

357. When you walk towards a light...
   a: The shadow behind you gets smaller
   b: The shadow behind you gets bigger
   c: The shadow behind you disappears
   d: Your shadow stays the same

358. What is special about a palm tree?
   a: No branches grow out of the trunk
   b: It's not technically a tree
   c: It can grow very tall
   d: All of the above

359. Melons grow under the ground.
   a: True **b:** False

360. Trees and plants produce oxygen.
   a: True **b:** False

361. What do you find on a prairie?
   a: Mainly trees
   b: Mainly grass
   c: Mainly flowers
   d: Mainly mountains

362. Which type of tree is the biggest?
   a: Oak **b:** Redwood
   c: Palm tree **d:** Plum tree

363. Plant roots are usually shorter in dry regions than in humid regions.
   a: True **b:** False

364 *Brain challenge*

Which type of plant closes its leaves when touched?

Touch-me-nots

365. If you add up the opposite sides of a dice, you always get 7.
a: True b: False

366. It is 6 o'clock. You have to be at school in two and a half hours. What time will it be then?
a: 7:30 b: 8:00
c: 8:30 d: 9:00

367. There are 14 shoes in the sports hall. How many children are going to do PE?
a: 4 b: 7 c: 8 d: 14

368. 15 is an even number.
a: True b: False

369. Which sum does NOT produce the answer 8?
a: 24 ÷ 3
b: 14 − 6
c: 7 + 2
d: 2 x 4

370. A hectometre is less than a metre.
a: True b: False

371. There are 15 minutes in a quarter of an hour.
a: True b: False

372. A pencil case costs £5, a school bag £15, a pencil £1 and a rubber £0.50. How much would you have to pay if you were to buy the school bag and the pencil?
a: £6 b: £15.50
c: £16 d: £21.50

373. How many sides does a cube have?
a: 4 b: 6
c: 8 d: 10

374. 13 does not belong in the following sequence: 4, 8, 13, 16, 20.
a: True b: False

Mathematics

Brain challenge

Which island do the Rapu Nui live on?

Easter Island

375. **What is someone who studies caves called?**
a: A speleologist b: A caveologist
c: A hololologist d: A boy scout

376. **What is special about the Dead Sea?**
a: The water is snow white in colour
b: You can float in the water without any effort c: The water is covered by unique water lilies d: It's very shallow – you can easily walk to the other side

377. **Oceania is the smallest continent.**
a: True b: False

378. **There is an earthquake somewhere on Earth every minute.**
a: True b: False

379. **The world's largest ocean is:**
a: The Pacific Ocean
b: The Indian Ocean
c: The Atlantic Ocean
d: The Arctic Ocean

380. **What is the Grand Canyon?**
a: One of the largest ravines in the world
b: One of the biggest mountains in the world
c: One of the biggest waterfalls in the world
d: One of the biggest volcanoes in the world

381. **Ebb means low water and flow means high water.**
a: True b: False

382. **Africa is smaller than North America.**
a: True b: False

383. **What pours out of a volcano during a volcanic explosion?**
a: Lever b: Loafer
c: Lava d: Vala

384. **It's always hot in a desert.**
a: True b: False

The Earth

386. People skated on animal bones in prehistoric times.
a: True b: False

387. Rugby is played with a round ball.
a: True b: False

388. The most expensive racing horse in the world was sold at auction for:
a: £900 b: £9,000
c: £90,000 d: £9,000,000

389. What cards can hockey players be given during a match?
a: Green, blue and yellow
b: Red, yellow and green
c: Blue, purple and red
d: Yellow, pink and blue

390. In football, the penalty spot is 50 metres from the goal.
a: True b: False

391. Snowboarding is an Olympic sport.
a: True b: False

392. How many players actively play on each team in basketball at any given time?
a: 5 b: 7
c: 11 d: 15

393. In water polo, the goal is underwater.
a: True b: False

394. Boxing matches are held in a 'ring'.
a: True b: False

395. Which sport involves the use of a 'shuttlecock'?
a: Discus throwing
b: Beach volleyball
c: Deep sea diving
d: Badminton

396 *Brain challenge*

What are the five colours of the Olympic rings?

Blue, yellow, black, green and red

Sport

397. You can ski on the sand in Dubai.
   a: True **b:** False

398. Which language is the most widely spoken on the planet?
   a: Spanish **b:** English
   c: Mandarin **d:** Arabic

399. The Great Wall of China is the longest wall in the world.
   a: True **b:** False

400. What is the name of the house where the American President lives?
   a: The Big House **b:** The King's House
   c: The Black House **d:** The White House

401. Which continent do most of the world's people live in?
   a: Africa **b:** Asia
   c: South America **d:** Oceania

402. Many Chinese people eat with sticks.
   a: True **b:** False

403. The Leaning Tower of Pisa is in Spain.
   a: True **b:** False

404. What nickname is given to people from New Zealand?
   a: Apples **b:** Pears
   c: Kiwis **d:** Bananas

405. Which dance is from South America?
   a: The tango **b:** The waltz
   c: The quickstep **d:** The clog dance

406. Hawaii is a state in the United States of America.
   a: True **b:** False

World travellers

Brain challenge

What do we call animals that can live both in the water and on land?

Amphibians

407. A swordfish is faster in the water than a cheetah on land.
a: True **b:** False

408. Which animal can live the longest?
a: The elephant **b:** The parrot
c: The giant tortoise **d:** The giant lizard

409. Which sleeping champion can sometimes sleep for 2 years at a time?
a: The sloth **b:** The lungfish
c: The leopard **d:** The bat

410. Mice can become pregnant as young as 4 weeks old.
a: True **b:** False

411. The ostrich is the fastest flightless bird in the world.
a: True **b:** False

412. Which mammal has the longest gestation period (the time that the mother is pregnant)?
a: The killer whale
b: The kangaroo
c: The orang-utan
d: The elephant

413. The penguin is the animal that can stay underwater the longest without breathing.
a: True **b:** False

414. The sloth is the slowest of all mammals.
a: True **b:** False

415. Which animal has the most teeth?
a: The lion **b:** The dolphin
c: The crocodile **d:** The elephant

416. The chimpanzee is the most intelligent animal in the world after humans.
a: True **b:** False

407: a 408: c 409: b 410: a 411: a 412: d 413: b 414: a 415: b 416: a

418. Only the black squares can be used in draughts.
a: True **b:** False

419. Uno...
a: Is a board game
b: Is a card game
c: Is a dice game
d: Is a single-player game

420. Which game has a king and a queen?
a: Monopoly **b:** Battleships
c: Draughts **d:** Chess

421. Frisbees are designed to float on water.
a: True **b:** False

422. Which game features ships?
a: Operation **b:** Who am I?
c: Battleships **d:** Yahtzee

423. Poker is a board game with coloured counters.
a: True **b:** False

424. What kind of game is Sudoku?
a: A card game **b:** A game of dice
c: A board game **d:** A number puzzle

425. Hide-and-seek is a game that was played in the Middle Ages.
a: True **b:** False

426. The yoyo was invented in 1800.
a: True **b:** False

427. What game involves jumping over other players' backs?
a: Frog hop
b: Grasshopper leap
c: Leapfrog
d: Kangaroo Boo

Games

428. The wheel was invented 1,000 years ago.
a: True **b:** False

429. In Germany, a mobile phone is called a 'Handy'.
a: True **b:** False

430. 'Eureka!' is sometimes proclaimed when a person resolves a difficult problem. What does this Greek word mean?
a: Hooray for me! **b:** I have found it!
c: If you think for long enough, you always find a solution! **d:** Listen to me!

431. A GPS can help you...
a: Find your way
b: Choose the best film
c: Clean your house
d: Beat a computer game

432. A microwave uses water to heat your food.
a: True **b:** False

433. Which animal is the computer pointing device named after?
a: A frog **b:** A mouse
c: A dog **d:** A cat

434. A computer program that can pose a threat to computers is a...
a: Pixel **b:** Virus
c: Contagion **d:** Caterpillar

435. A Philips screwdriver can be used to screw any kind of screw into a wall.
a: True **b:** False

436. What was the very first zip used for?
a: Bags **b:** Jackets
c: Trousers **d:** Boots

437. You can listen to music on gramophone records.
a: True **b:** False

Eureka!

Technology and inventions

438. Picasso invented the piano.
a: True b: False

439. Which of the following is NOT an instrument?
a: Friction drum b: Singing saw
c: Wind gong d: Dooda flute

440. A ukulele is a type of...
a: Small flute b: Small piano
c: Small guitar d: Small drum

441. The 'pop' in pop music is short for 'popular'.
a: True b: False

442. The first flute was made 100 years ago.
a: True b: False

443. How many keys does a piano usually have?
a: 22 b: 44
c: 66 d: 88

444. When you play a theremin, you don't touch the instrument itself.
a: True b: False

445. The didgeridoo (a wind instrument) is:
a: Long b: Short
c: Round (like a ball) d: Square

446. Which of the following is NOT a percussion instrument?
a: Djembe b: Cymbal
c: Oboe d: Tambourine

447. When improvising, a musician always knows exactly how he will play the piece beforehand.
a: True b: False

Music

448. A year on Mars is almost twice as long as a year on Earth.
a: True b: False

449. The Sun is the largest star in our star system.
a: True b: False

450. Why don't you see stars in the sky during the day?
a: The stars are on the other side of the world during the day
b: Stars don't shine during the day
c: You can't see stars during the day because the Sun is so bright
d: The Earth is too far from the stars during the day for them to be visible

451. How many times would the Earth fit into the planet Jupiter?
a: 19 times b: 468 times
c: 1,321 times d: 11 million times

452. The Sun is the farthest star from the Earth.
a: True b: False

453. What was the name of the first dog in space?
a: Laika b: Bobby
c: Idéfix d: Dommel

454. The word astronaut is from Greek and means 'star sailor'.
a: True b: False

455. Which planet is not named after a god or goddess?
a: Earth b: Mars
c: Uranus d: Venus

456. How long does it take to travel from the Earth to the Moon?
a: A few hours
b: A few days
c: A few weeks
d: A few months

457. The best time to see a shooting star is on a cloudy night.
a: True b: False

Space

458. A phoenix is a type of mythical bird.
a: True b: False

459. Which Smurf wears a red hat?
a: Grouchy Smurf
b: Smurfette
c: Brainy Smurf
d: Big Smurf

460. What is Donald Duck's girlfriend called?
a: Minnie b: Daisy
c: Lizzie d: Clarabella

461. Unicorns are always black.
a: True b: False

462. The main character in The Lion King is called Simba.
a: True b: False

463. How many Teletubbies are there?
a: 2 b: 4
c: 6 d: 10

468
Brain challenge

What is Peter Pan's dog called?

Nana

464. Bambi is in love with ...
a: Thumper
b: Flower
c: Faline
d: Owl

465. The Greeks are Asterix and Obelix's enemies.
a: True b: False

466. Fiona is Shrek's girlfriend.
a: True b: False

467. How many times does Aladdin have to rub the lamp to make a wish?
a: 1 b: 2
c: 3 d: 4

Fairy tales and fantasy

458: a 459: d 460: b 461: b 462: a 463: b 464: c 465: b 466: a 467: c

469. If you want to measure air pressure, you use...
a: A thermometer
b: A hygrometer
c: A barometer
d: A hectometer

470. What is a child's first set of teeth called?
a: Butter teeth
b: Milk teeth
c: Egg teeth
d: Cheese teeth

471. Humans cannot survive without oxygen.
a: True **b:** False

472. Light travels faster than sound.
a: True **b:** False

473. It is possible to shatter a glass using only your voice.
a: True **b:** False

474. Dogs hear...
a: Mainly higher tones better than humans
b: Mainly lower tones better than humans
c: Both higher and lower tones better than humans
d: Exactly the same as humans

475. The bang that you hear when a balloon bursts is caused by the sudden release of a lot of air.
a: True **b:** False

476. What is a plastic soft drink bottle called?
a: A POT bottle
b: A PIT bottle
c: A PET bottle
d: A PUT bottle

477. A balloon filled with helium gas rises because helium is lighter than air.
a: True **b:** False

478. Gravity is stronger on the Moon than on Earth.
a: True **b:** False

Science

479. **When you knock into something, first you feel the contact with your skin, then the pain.**
    a: True b: False

480. **How often do you breathe in and out each day?**
    a: 200 times
    b: 2,000 times
    c: 20,000 times
    d: 20 million times

481. **Both your lungs are the same size.**
    a: True b: False

482. **The blood in your body always flows in the same direction.**
    a: True b: False

483. **How fast does the hair on your head grow?**
    a: Around 1 cm a day
    b: Around 1 cm a week
    c: Around 1 cm a month
    d: Around 1 cm a year

Brain challenge

What kind of scientist studies plants?

A botanist

484. **What do we call the journey that food takes through the body?**
    a: Food journey b: Digestion
    c: Food trip d: Meal flow

485. **It's easier to talk when inhaling than exhaling.**
    a: True b: False

486. **Where in the body is the cochlea found?**
    a: Your nose b: Your inner ear
    c: Your intestines d: Your brain

487. **Through which part of the body does blood not flow?**
    a: Your nose b: Your bottom
    c: Your toes d: Your teeth

488. **Muscles can only pull on bones, not push.**
    a: True b: False

Biology

500

Brain challenge

What do we call the outermost leaves of a flower?

Sepals

490. Plants make oxygen as a by-product of which process?
a: Oxygen prosthesis **b:** Light therapy
c: Video conferencing **d:** Photosynthesis

491. What is sunflower oil made from?
a: The leaves of sunflowers
b: The stems of sunflowers
c: The seeds of sunflowers
d: All the parts of the sunflower

492. You won't find snow anywhere in Africa.
a: True **b:** False

493. Silk is made by silkworms.
a: True **b:** False

494. How do you tell the age of a tree?
a: By counting the number of leaves on it
b: By counting the number of branches on it
c: By measuring the thickness of it
d: By felling the tree and counting the number of rings in the trunk

495. Just like people, trees stop growing at a certain age.
a: True **b:** False

496. Mangoes grow...
a: On high trees **b:** On low bushes
c: Underground **d:** Just above the ground

497. The outermost layer of a tree trunk is called bark.
a: True **b:** False

498. There is a much greater chance of rain with high cloud cover than with low cloud cover.
a: True **b:** False

499. Where does liquorice come from?
a: The branches of the liquorice tree
b: The roots of the liquorice tree
c: The flowers of the liquorice tree
d: Liquorice is not a natural product – it is made in factories

Nature

501. 20 x 0 = 20
a: True b: False

502. Which sum produces the highest answer?
a: 4 + 2 b: 4 x 2
c: 4 – 2 d: 4 ÷ 2

503. A restaurant has 5 tables each with 5 places. How many people can eat there at once?
a: 10 b: 15
c: 25 d: 50

504. A football team comprises 11 players, 7 of whom are girls. How many boys are there in the team?
a: 2 b: 4
c: 6 d: 8

505. 5,000 metres is half a kilometre.
a: True b: False

506. You can't throw higher than a 12 with 2 dice.
a: True b: False

507. Hungry? You have 3 eggs. You need 6 to make pancakes. How many eggs do you need to buy?
a: 1 b: 2 c: 3 d: 4

508. Three brothers are going on holiday. Each is taking 2 pairs of shorts and 1 pair of swimming shorts with them. How many pairs of shorts are they taking altogether?
a: 3 b: 6 c: 9 d: 12

509. There are 299 days in a year.
a: True b: False

510. Two £2 coins and a £10 note make £15.
a: True b: False

511 *Brain challenge*

How many seconds are there in an hour?

3,600

Mathematics

512. How long does it take the Earth to orbit the Sun?
a: 1 day **b:** 1 week **c:** 1 month **d:** 1 year

513. Less than half of the Earth is covered by water.
a: True **b:** False

514. An archaeologist is someone who studies the relics, ruins and other physical remains of past cultures.
a: True **b:** False

515. What is the Sahara?
a: The largest sand desert on Earth
b: The largest rock desert on Earth
c: The largest salt desert on Earth
d: The largest ice desert on Earth

516. Day and night are the same length during the equinox.
a: True **b:** False

517. What is the capital of France?
a: Berlin **b:** Paris
c: Stockholm **d:** Madrid

518. What is another name for the Dead Sea?
a: The Black Sea **b:** The Red Sea
c: The Salt Sea **d:** The Sweet Sea

519. Agate is a precious stone.
a: True **b:** False

520. Canada has a larger surface area than the United States of America.
a: True **b:** False

521. Where do you find the Midnight Sun, i.e. when the Sun doesn't set for weeks?
a: Only at the North Pole
b: Only at the South Pole
c: At the North and South Poles
d: Always at different places around the world

The Earth

Brain challenge

532

In which sport can you win the Stanley Cup?

ice hockey

522. How many kilometres do runners have to run in a marathon?
a: More than 2 b: More than 22
c: More than 42 d: More than 82

523. The Winter and Summer Olympic Games comprise the same sports.
a: True b: False

524. Cross-country skis are longer than normal skis.
a: True b: False

525. When is a red card given in football?
a: When a player has to leave the field
b: When a player arrives on the field
c: When a goal has been scored
d: When a player is injured

526. Which animal's name represents the swimming stroke that involves moving both arms at the same time?
a: The dolphin b: The butterfly
c: The bee d: The dragonfly

527. Golf is played with 'handicaps'.
a: True b: False

528. Sumo wrestling is a sport for skinny people.
a: True b: False

529. A 'strike' in bowling is when...
a: You knock over all the pins in one go
b: You knock over all the pins in two goes
c: You haven't knocked any pins after two goes
d: You knock over the far right and far left pins in one go

530. What is the highest possible achievement at the Olympic Games?
a: A gold cup
b: A silver cup
c: A gold medal
d: A silver medal

531. The world record for the high jump is 2.44 m.
a: True b: False

533. How many arms do starfish have?
a: 2 b: 5
c: 8 d: 15

534. All animals that live in the sea can swim.
a: True b: False

535. A dolphin is a mammal.
a: True b: False

536. When a shark stops swimming...
a: It sinks
b: It floats to the top
c: It stays in the same place
d: It goes around in circles

537. A beaver's front teeth are:
a: Green
b: White
c: Black
d: Orange

538. If an octopus loses an arm, a new one does not grow in its place.
a: True b: False

539. Jellyfish are largely made up of water.
a: True b: False

540. Walruses steer...
a: With their heads
b: With their tails
c: With their dorsal fins
d: With their stomachs

541. How many legs does a crab have?
a: 6 b: 8 c: 10 d: 12

542. Cygnets (baby swans) are always white.
a: True b: False

Water animals

543. Which language is spoken in Argentina?
a: Italian **b:** Spanish
c: Portuguese **d:** English

544. Which fruit is eaten at 12 o'clock on New Year's Eve in Spain?
a: Strawberries **b:** Grapes
c: Apples **d:** Plums

545. Almost twice as many people live in China as do in all of Europe.
a: True **b:** False

546. New Year is celebrated earlier in Australia than in America.
a: True **b:** False

547. Which is the biggest country in the world?
a: Russia **b:** China
c: Canada **d:** Australia

548. What are the two official languages of Canada?
a: Spanish and English
b: French and German
c: Russian and Chinese
d: English and French

549. Las Vegas is a city famous for gambling.
a: True **b:** False

550. Chickens are holy animals in India.
a: True **b:** False

551. What is the currency of Brazil?
a: Yen **b:** Real **c:** Crown **d:** Peso

552. What is the English word for the currency of Norway, Sweden and Denmark?
a: The crown **b:** The mark
c: The euro **d:** The lira

553 *Brain challenge*

Which continent contains the most countries?

Africa

World travellers

Brain challenge

Which well-known wind instrument originated from Australian Aboriginals?

The didgeridoo

554. The first digital computer was...
a: Smaller than a mouse
b: As big as a book
c: As big as a car
d: Bigger than a classroom

555. Leonardo da Vinci invented the wheel.
a: True b: False

556. The radio was invented before the television.
a: True b: False

557. In which country was paper invented?
a: America b: China
c: Turkey d: Russia

558. Which object is made mainly from rubber?
a: A mirror b: A pencil
c: A car tyre d: Trousers

559. A round building is sturdier than a triangular-shaped building.
a: True b: False

560. The dice was invented around 5,000 years ago.
a: True b: False

561. What do we call a person who designs buildings?
a: An anthropologist b: An archaeologist
c: An astrologist d: An architect

562. Which direction does a compass always point?
a: North b: East
c: South d: West

563. Morse code is a system of transmitting letters and numbers as dots and stripes.
a: True b: False

Technology and inventions

554: d 555: b 556: a 557: b 558: c 559: b 560: a 561: d 562: a 563: a

565. Which game requires a length of string?
a: Diabolo **b:** Juggling
c: Roulette **d:** Bridge

566. Two armies face each other in Stratego.
a: True **b:** False

567. Solitaire is played with 4 or more people.
a: True **b:** False

568. What is another name for tic-tac-toe?
a: Squares and circles
b: Crosses and noughts
c: Noughts and crosses
d: Three in a row

569. Which of the following is a not card game?
a: Klaberjass **b:** Rummikub
c: Halli Galli **d:** Uno

570. You need a blindfold to play Pin the Tail on the Donkey.
a: True **b:** False

571. Marbles is one of the oldest children's games.
a: True **b:** False

572. In which game can you end up in prison?
a: Game of the Goose
b: Ludo
c: Dominoes
d: Connect Four

573. Which game involves solving a murder mystery?
a: The Game of Life
b: The Settlers of Catan
c: Pitfall
d: Cluedo

574. Operation involves collecting a patient's body parts.
a: True **b:** False

575 Brain challenge

How many dots are there on a dice?

21

Games

Brain challenge

What is a morning love song called?

An aubade

576. A solo is performed by...
a: 1 person b: 2 people
c: 3 people d: Any number of people

577. A piano has strings.
a: True b: False

578. Which country does the didgeridoo come from?
a: Canada
b: Argentina
c: China
d: Australia

579. The sound made by an electric guitar is heard through a loudspeaker.
a: True b: False

580. People were making music even in prehistoric times.
a: True b: False

581. Plucking is done:
a: On the trumpet b: On a piano
c: On a guitar d: On a xylophone

582. You can play a drum...
a: With your hands
b: With your fingers
c: With sticks
d: All of the above

583. Someone with a soprano voice sings lower than someone with a bass voice.
a: True b: False

584. Men usually sing lower than women.
a: True b: False

585. Which type of flute is the smallest?
a: The Western concert flute
b: The piccolo
c: The bass flute
d: The alto flute

Music

597 Brain challenge

Laika the dog was not the first animal sent into space. What kind of animal was the first?

fruit flies

587. All of the planets in our solar system orbit the Sun.
a: True **b:** False

588. What is the name of our galaxy?
a: The Star Watch
b: The Gold Line
c: The Light Route
d: The Milky Way

589. When you look outside at night, you often see stars twinkling or blinking because...
a: The stars are so far from the Earth
b: The stars are almost 'dead' and are about to go out
c: The air above the Earth is moving
d: Stars sometimes shine more or less than usual

590. A shooting star looks like a streak of light in the sky.
a: True **b:** False

591. Planets never follow the same trajectory through space.
a: True **b:** False

592. What do spacemen do with their urine in space?
a: They turn it into a cleaning product
b: They turn it into drinking water
c: They turn it into a type of fuel
d: Nothing – they pour it out into space

593. Which planet is no longer considered a planet?
a: Pluto **b:** Uranus
c: Mercury **d:** Venus

594. The Moon appears to produce light because it reflects the Sun's rays.
a: True **b:** False

595. Stars are always yellow.
a: True **b:** False

596. What is a Supernova?
a: A giant planet
b: An exploding star
c: A very young star
d: A storm of shooting stars

598. **Who does NOT live underwater?**
a: Nemo **b:** SpongeBob
c: Gyro Gearloose **d:** King Neptune

599. **Obelix fell into the magic potion when he was small.**
a: True **b:** False

600. **Which fruit poisons Snow White?**
a: An apple **b:** A pear
c: A banana **d:** A grape

601. **Cinderella pricks her finger on a spinning wheel and falls asleep.**
a: True **b:** False

602. **Dragons spit fire.**
a: True **b:** False

603. **Which superhero looks like a bat?**
a: Spiderman **b:** Batman
c: Superman **d:** Iron Man

604. **What is the dinosaur called in Toy Story?**
a: Buzz **b:** Rex
c: Dino **d:** Sid

605. **Tarzan was raised by tigers.**
a: True **b:** False

606. **Donald Duck's sailor outfit is blue.**
a: True **b:** False

607. **Which girl does NOT marry a prince?**
a: Snow White
b: Cinderella
c: Pocahontas
d: Sleeping Beauty

Fairy tales and fantasy

608. **Which unit or units can be used to measure temperature?**
a: Celsius **b:** Fahrenheit
c: Kelvin **d:** All of the above

609. **When metal heats up...**
a: It expands, so it gets bigger
b: It shrinks, so it get smaller
c: It breaks
d: Nothing happens

610. **The very first trains ran on steam.**
a: True **b:** False

611. **What did the Greek inventor Archimedes discover?**
a: That water rises or is displaced when something is placed in it
b: That helium is lighter than air
c: How raindrops occur
d: That the Earth is round

612. **Boiling water turns into steam.**
a: True **b:** False

613. **What colour do you find at the top of a rainbow?**
a: Red **b:** Yellow **c:** Green **d:** Blue

614. **You never hear echoes in a tunnel.**
a: True **b:** False

615. **Your voice sounds different to you than it does to other people.**
a: True **b:** False

616. **What is the best conductor of electricity?**
a: Copper **b:** Gold **c:** Iron **d:** Wood

617. **When ice melts it turns into snow.**
a: True **b:** False

619. What colour is your brain?
a: Grey b: Blue c: Pink d: Green

620. The best way of ensuring that a bruise doesn't spread is to put something cold on it.
a: True b: False

621. Where does the rumbling noise you sometimes hear when you're hungry come from?
a: Your stomach b: Your lungs
c: Your intestines d: Your throat

622. Where in your body can you find a hammer?
a: In your hands b: In your toes
c: In your stomach d: In your ear

623. There are tiny hairs in your nose that filter the air you inhale.
a: True b: False

624. A baby has as much blood in its body as an adult.
a: True b: False

625. What is the average human body temperature?
a: 25 degrees centigrade
b: 31 degrees centigrade
c: 37 degrees centigrade
d: 48 degrees centigrade

626. Every human, including twins, has unique fingerprints.
a: True b: False

627. When you sleep, your brain becomes inactive.
a: True b: False

628. Twins that look the same are:
a: Zerozygotic twins b: Monozygotic twins
c: Dizygotic twins d: Trizygotic twins

629 *Brain challenge*

How many hearts does an earthworm have?

5 pairs, 10 in total

Brain challenge

640

How many centimetres are there in a kilometre?

100,000

630. If you can walk 10 kilometres in 2 hours, you can walk 5 kilometres in 1 hour.
a: True **b:** False

631. It is 3 o'clock in the afternoon. You have to sleep in 5 hours. That will be:
a: 7 o'clock in the evening **b:** Half past 7 in the evening **c:** 8 o'clock in the evening **d:** 9 o'clock in the evening

632. You collect stamps. You have 7. Your best friend has 6. How many stamps do the two of you have together?
a: 11 **b:** 12 **c:** 13 **d:** 14

633. 4 x 5 = 20.
a: True **b:** False

634. Complete the sequence: 4, 8, 12, ?
a: 14 **b:** 16 **c:** 18 **d:** 20

635. You've scored 6 points in a game. Joe has scored half as many as you and Mary has scored twice as many as Joe. How many points does Mary have?
a: 3 **b:** 6 **c:** 12 **d:** 24

636. One bread roll costs £0,20 at the bakery. You have £1. How many bread rolls can you buy?
a: 1 **b:** 3 **c:** 5 **d:** 10

637. 2 x 15 = 30
a: True **b:** False

638. A rabbit eats 2 carrots. A horse eats 4. A donkey eats 6. How many carrots do they eat in total?
a: 6 **b:** 8 **c:** 10 **d:** 12

639. If you throw 3 dice at the same time, you will always get higher than a 5.
a: True **b:** False

Mathematics

641. No flowers grow in the desert.
   a: True **b:** False

642. Big trees are sometimes called 'mammoth trees'.
   a: True **b:** False

643. Insects ensure that plants can reproduce, but how?
   a: They transport nectar between plants
   b: They transport pollen between plants
   c: They transport pistils between plants
   d: They transport stamens between plants

644. No trees grow above a certain height in the mountains. What do we call that point?
   a: The tree line
   b: The grow line
   c: The grass line
   d: The plant line

645. Grass grows faster in winter than in summer.
   a: True **b:** False

646. Tea is made from beans, just like coffee and cocoa.
   a: True **b:** False

647. Which of the following is NOT a citrus fruit?
   a: Orange **b:** Lemon
   c: Banana **d:** Grapefruit

648. What do we call the seeds of pine trees?
   a: Pinacolada **b:** Pine cones
   c: Pineapples **d:** Pine nuts

649. Chewing gum used to be made from natural gum. This comes from...
   a: The sap of certain trees
   b: Underground
   c: The fruit of gum trees
   d: Factories

650. The best place to grow mushrooms is in dark and damp conditions.
   a: True **b:** False

Nature

656. Lava is called magma before it comes out of a volcano.
a: True **b:** False

657. There are countries that lie below sea level.
a: True **b:** False

658. Which continent is Argentina in?
a: Africa **b:** Asia
c: Oceania **d:** South America

651. Which scale is used to measure the force of an earthquake?
a: The Rector Scale **b:** The Richter Scale
c: The Biscay Scale **d:** The Vesuvius Scale

659. What is the name of the longest river in the world?
a: The Amazon **b:** The Nile
c: The Rhine **d:** The Niger

652. Vatican City is the smallest country in the world.
a: True **b:** False

660. Portugal is in Asia.
a: True **b:** False

653. It never rains in the Sahara.
a: True **b:** False

654. Which South American country has the colour green in its flag?
a: Argentina **b:** Chile
c: Brazil **d:** Peru

655. What colour is the breast of a robin?
a: Red **b:** Blue
c: Green **d:** Black

661 *Brain challenge*

How many rivers are there in Saudi Arabia?

0

The Earth

662. Penguins live on the South Pole, but not on the North Pole.
a: True b: False

663. How big are a giant octopus's eyes?
a: As big as a marble
b: As big as a tennis ball
c: As big as a football
d: As big as a kangaroo ball

664. Flamingos prefer to stand on two legs in the water.
a: True b: False

665. Where does a mother crocodile keep her eggs safe?
a: She lays them in a deserted duck or swan nest b: She holds them in her mouth until they hatch c: She hides them in the bushes d: She buries them in the sand

666. Male ducks do not get to know their own children.
a: True b: False

667. The ancestors of the whale had legs and lived on land.
a: True b: False

668. What kind of animal is a piranha?
a: A crocodile b: A fish
c: A snake d: A duck

669. Where are walrus babies born?
a: In the grass
b: On the ice
c: In the water
d: In a nest

670. A young seal that loses its mother is called a 'crier'.
a: True b: False

671. Adult pandas can't swim.
a: True b: False

Animals

672. Kin-Ball is played with a very small ball.
 a: True **b:** False

673. Which martial art did not originate in Japan?
 a: Judo **b:** Karate
 c: Jujitsu **d:** Taekwondo

674. Which flag is flown for the winner of a car race?
 a: A red and blue striped flag
 b: A black and white chequered flag
 c: A gold flag
 d: A green flag

675. A horse and a beam are used in gymnastics.
 a: True **b:** False

676. The same rules apply in ice hockey and field hockey.
 a: True **b:** False

677. What object do discus throwers throw?
 a: A ball **b:** A flat disc
 c: A javelin **d:** An arrow

678. Weightlifting is a sport that is part of the Winter Olympics.
 a: True **b:** False

679. Honkbal is the Dutch word for baseball.
 a: True **b:** False

680. How often are the Summer Olympics held?
 a: Every year **b:** Every two years
 c: Every four years **d:** Every ten years

681. What does a gymnast rub on his hands before swinging on the rings?
 a: Oil **b:** Water **c:** Salt
 d: Magnesium carbonate

Sport

692 *Brain challenge*

What is the name of the widest river in the world?

The Amazon

682. Everybody dresses up as a clown during Carnival in Brazil.
a: True b: False

683. The most widely-spoken languages in South America are:
a: English and French
b: English and Spanish
c: Spanish and Portuguese
d: German and French

684. What is Easter Island famous for?
a: Only animals live there b: It has gigantic statues all along its coastline c: A type of rabbit that can lay eggs lives there d: It is not an island at all

685. The Queen of England is also the queen of...
a: America b: Kenya
c: Australia d: India

686. Sombreros (large Mexican hats) are worn when someone is sombre or sad.
a: True b: False

687. Which shape features on the European flag?
a: Triangles b: Cubes
c: Ovals d: Stars

688. What material is the Eiffel Tower made from?
a: Wood b: Iron
c: Stone d: Plastic

689. There are no pyramids in Mexico.
a: True b: False

690. Many African flags feature the colour green because there are many forests in Africa.
a: True b: False

691. How long is the Great Wall of China?
a: Almost 8.9 kilometres
b: Almost 89 kilometres
c: Almost 890 kilometres
d: Almost 8,900 kilometres

World travellers

693. Bert and Ernie are characters in Sesame Street.
a: True **b:** False

694. What type of animal is Garfield?
a: A dog **b:** A cat
c: A mouse **d:** A frog

695. According to the Chinese, dragons bring good luck.
a: True **b:** False

696. A werewolf is a person who can turn into a wolf.
a: True **b:** False

697. Who is Gretel left in the forest and locked in a witch's house with?
a: Her brother Gunter
b: Her brother Hansel
c: Her cousin Karel
d: Her cousin Jack

698. What is Obelix's favourite food?
a: Carrots **b:** Apples
c: Wild boar **d:** Chicken

699. In Tom and Jerry, Tom is the mouse.
a: True **b:** False

700. Which famous mythical creature do you find at the port in Copenhagen?
a: A gnome **b:** An elf
c: A mermaid **d:** A troll

701. What is the Smurfs' enemy called?
a: Dracula **b:** Darius
c: Gargamel **d:** Mario

702. A lion and a tiger try to lead Pinocchio astray.
a: True **b:** False

703 *Brain challenge*

Which fairytale features a mad hatter?

Alice in Wonderland

Fairy tales and fantasy

693: a 694: b 695: a 696: a 697: b 698: c 699: b 700: c 701: c 702: b

704. A kettle drum is a wind instrument.
  a: True **b:** False

705. A string orchestra comprises mainly trumpets and saxophones.
  a: True **b:** False

706. A song usually comprises 1 chorus and several...
  a: Verses
  b: Arias
  c: Chapters
  d: Paragraphs

707. A troubadour is...
  a: A musical instrument
  b: A musical piece
  c: A travelling singer
  d: A children's orchestra

708. Mozart wrote his first piece when he was 5 years old.
  a: True **b:** False

709. What does someone who sings 'a capella' do?
  a: Sings and dances at the same time
  b: Sings without instrumental accompaniment
  c: Sings off key
  d: Sings very low

714 Brain challenge

What is a mazurka?

A dance

710. What is a quartet?
  a: A musical piece with 4 musical instruments
  b: A musical piece lasting 15 minutes
  c: A group of 4 musicians
  d: An instrument with 4 strings

711. Every stave starts with a clef.
  a: True **b:** False

712. A tuba only produces high notes.
  a: True **b:** False

713. What types of wind instruments are there?
  a: Woodwind and brass
  b: Silver and gold
  c: Plastic and woodwind
  d: All of the above

715. Which country was Yuri Gagarin (the first man in space) from?
a: America **b:** China **c:** Russia **d:** Argentina

716. Both a dog and a chimpanzee have been in space.
a: True **b:** False

717. The oldest astronaut was John Glenn, who went to space at the age of 77.
a: True **b:** False

718. If you could jump one metre on Earth, how high could you jump on the Moon?
a: 2 metres **b:** 4 metres
c: 6 metres **d:** 8 metres

719. Which planet has the shortest days?
a: Mars **b:** Earth
c: Mercury **d:** Jupiter

720. The Sun and the Moon are the same size.
a: True **b:** False

721. Planets produce light.
a: True **b:** False

722. What is a shooting star?
a: A small piece of stone that enters the Earth's atmosphere very fast and burns
b: A small piece of ice that enters the Earth's atmosphere very fast and melts

725 Brain challenge

How many months does it take for the Moon to orbit the Earth once?

c: A star that has exploded and now floats through space
d: An old star that has burnt up

723. When an astronaut prepares to sleep in space...
a: He lays down on a bed, like he would on Earth, and doesn't float away
b: He has to strap himself into a sleeping bag so that he doesn't float around
c: He floats through the spaceship, until he wakes up
d: None of the above. You don't need to sleep in space

724. The words astronaut, cosmonaut and taikonaut all mean the same thing.
a: True **b:** False

Space

726. Anthropoid apes have...
a: No hair b: No tail
c: No nails d: No ears

727. The first humans were born in the time of the dinosaurs.
a: True b: False

728. Many mammoths used to have...
a: A long and woolly coat
b: Feathers
c: Large scales
d: A coat of sharp spikes

729. The dodo was a large flightless bird.
a: True b: False

730. All dinosaurs ate meat.
a: True b: False

731. The name 'dinosaur' comes from...
a: Greek b: Latin
c: Chinese d: Arabic

732. Which animal is not a dinosaur?
a: The Tyrannosaurus rex
b: The Paradontaris
c: The Triceratops
d: The Stegosaurus

733. There were hedgehogs in the time of the dinosaurs.
a: True b: False

734. A turtle usually lays only a single egg at a time.
a: True b: False

735. To which family does the dodo belong?
a: The ostrich b: The turkey
c: The pheasant d: The dove

Extinct and
threatend animals

736. You can rinse grease off your hands without using soap.
a: True b: False

737. What were sundials once used for?
a: To predict the weather
b: To find due north
c: To tell the time
d: To tell what year it was

738. If you bounce a ball on the ground, the ball flattens a little.
a: True b: False

739. If you were to drop a hammer and a feather on the Moon at the same time...
a: The hammer would hit the ground before the feather
b: The feather would hit the ground before the hammer
c: The feather and the hammer would hit the ground at the same time
d: The feather and the hammer would not hit the ground

740. What are the white streaks that planes leave behind in the air?
a: Chalk b: Water vapour
c: Fuel d: Electricity

741. What do we call a person who studies the climate?
a: A meteorologist b: A speleologist
c: A physiologist d: A cardiologist

742. How hot can a flash of lightning get?
a: 30 degrees Celsius
b: 300 degrees Celsius
c: 30,000 degrees Celsius
d: 3 million degrees Celsius

743. Diamond is the strongest mineral on Earth.
a: True b: False

744. What prize can you win if you make an important scientific discovery?
a: The Newton Prize
b: The Nobel Prize
c: The Neutron Prize
d: The Quark Prize

745. At what temperature does ice melt?
a: -5 degrees Celsius
b: 0 degrees Celsius
c: 5 degrees Celsius
d: 100 degrees Celsius

746 *Brain challenge*

Which unit is used to measure the power of electric current?

Amperes

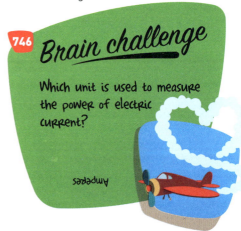

Science

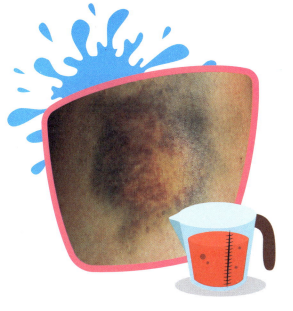

751. How many litres of blood flow through an adult body?
a: 1 litre b: 3 litres c: 5 litres d: 7 litres

752. A bruise is a small injury under the skin.
a: True b: False

753. Where is the thickest skin on your body?
a: On your cheeks
b: On your bottom
c: On your palms
d: On the soles of your feet

754. Which colour is NOT a colour of human or animal blood?
a: Green b: Red
c: White d: Black

755. The body is largely made up of water.
a: True b: False

756. Sweating makes you warmer.
a: True b: False

747. Your heart is roughly as big as...
a: Your head b: Your finger
c: Your lower leg d: Your fist

748. Your muscles make up around half of your bodyweight.
a: True b: False

749. Most people can touch their elbow with their tongue.
a: True b: False

750. Where in your body is your funny bone?
a: Your ear b: Your upper arm
c: Your wrist d: Your shoulder

Biology

757. Foxes bury their leftover food so that they can eat it later.
a: True **b:** False

758. Newborn hedgehogs already have sharp spikes.
a: True **b:** False

759. An owl's eyes are...
a: On the front of its head
b: On the back of its head
c: On the sides of its head
d: On the top of its head

760. Pigs like to roll in mud because...
a: They'd rather be dirty than clean
b: It relieves itching of the back
c: They love the smell of mud
d: It cools them down

761. Rabbits hide in a warren under the ground during the day.
a: True **b:** False

762. Foxes bark.
a: True **b:** False

763. How often are sheep sheared?
a: Once a week **b:** Once a month
c: Once a year **d:** Once in their lifetime

764. When hunting, a lioness...
a: Takes her young with her
b: Hides her young in the grass and leaves
c: Lets the father look after the young
d: Sends her young off hunting by themselves

765. A rabbit can growl.
a: True **b:** False

766. Hyena packs are led by a female.
a: True **b:** False

Wild animals

767. Which tree is NOT a pine tree?
a: Pine b: Spruce c: Larch d: Beech

768. The largest tropical rainforest on Earth is the Amazon region in South America.
a: True b: False

769. What are the rings in a tree trunk called?
a: Trunk rings b: Year rings
c: Growth rings d: Bark rings

770. Rice only grows in hot, humid places.
a: True b: False

771. An arboretum is a park where many different types of trees grow.
a: True b: False

772. If you look outside on a summer's morning, the grass might be wet, even though it hasn't rained. The water droplets on the grass are called...
a: Haze b: Mist
c: Dew d: Few

773. We say that a four-leaf clover brings good luck because few clovers have four leaves. How many leaves do most clovers have?
a: 2 b: 3 c: 5 d: 6

774. Young sunflowers...
a: Close their leaves in bright sunlight
b: Follow the sun from sunrise to sunset
c: Never face in the direction of the sun
d: Always face straight upwards, sun or no sun

775. Some plants eat insects.
a: True b: False

776. Bamboo shoots are hollow on the inside.
a: True b: False

777 *Brain challenge*

What do we call the petrified remains of a plant or animal?

fossils

778. Ducks keep their eyes open when they sleep.
a: True b: False

779. Parrots are silent when they're bored.
a: True b: False

780. Where do peacocks prefer to sleep?
a: On the ground b: In a hole
c: In a tree d: In a cave

781. Which part of the body can an owl not move?
a: Its head b: Its eyes
c: Its legs d: Its wings

782. A male dove is called a cock.
a: True b: False

788 *Brain challenge*

What was the first song ever to be sung in space?

Happy birthday

783. Penguins are good fliers.
a: True b: False

784. Which ducks make quacking noises?
a: Only female ducks
b: Only male ducks
c: Male and female ducks
d: Neither

785. Sometimes falcons seem to stay at one spot in the air. We call this...
a: Hanging b: Being lazy
c: Hovering d: Sulking

786. The skin that hangs from a turkey's forehead is called a 'snood'.
a: True b: False

787. A bat is a bird.
a: True b: False

Birds

789. Pyramid shapes are made up of triangles.
a: True **b:** False

790. A carton of milk costs £2. You pay with £5. How much change do you receive?
a: £1 **b:** £2
c: £3 **d:** £4

791. How many sides do 2 hexagons have in total?
a: 2 **b:** 6 **c:** 12 **d:** 18

792. 6 + 8 is as much as 18 − 4.
a: True **b:** False

793. How many corners does a cube have?
a: 2 **b:** 4 **c:** 6 **d:** 8

794. 15 − 7 = 8
a: True **b:** False

795. You have 6 apples. You give one to your sister and you eat one yourself. How many apples do you have left?
a: 3 **b:** 4 **c:** 5 **d:** 6

796. What can you make by placing two squares next to each other?
a: A diamond
b: A rectangle
c: A circle
d: A trapezium

797. A year has 13 months.
a: True **b:** False

798. Your neighbour has 6 crayons. You have twice as many. How many do you have?
a: 10 **b:** 12 **c:** 14 **d:** 16

799 Brain challenge

How many squares are there on a chess board?

64

Mathematics

800. Basketballs are filled with sand.
a: True **b:** False

801. In netball, you can touch the ball with your foot as well as your hands.
a: True **b:** False

802. 'Headspinning' is turning around in circles on your head. What is the world record?
a: 15 turns a minute
b: 75 turns a minute
c: 135 turns a minute
d: 545 turns a minute

803. In which sport are penalty corners taken?
a: Field hockey **b:** Tennis
c: Volleyball **d:** Horse riding

804. Both American footballs and rugby balls are shaped like an egg.
a: True **b:** False

805. The discus thrown by female discus throwers is lighter than that thrown by male discuss throwers.
a: True **b:** False

806. How long is the swimming pool that is used for the Olympic Games?
a: 15 metres **b:** 25 metres
c: 50 metres **d:** 100 metres

807. Which sport is NOT practised in or on the water?
a: Sailing **b:** Snorkelling **c:** Kayaking **d:** Polo

808. A common word for the goalkeeper in football is 'goalie'.
a: True **b:** False

809. The words helmet and habit are used in swimming.
a: True **b:** False

810

Brain challenge

How many scoring areas are there on a dartboard?

82

811. **Tomatoes originally come from South America.**
a: True b: False

812. **What is the skirt called that Scottish men wear at special events?**
a: A kilt b: A kult c: A kolt d: A kelt

813. **What was a sign of social status among the ancient people on Easter Island?**
a: By the length of his nose
b: By the length of his ears
c: By the length of his toes
d: By the length of his hair

814. **The first voyages of discovery were made without world maps or compasses.**
a: True b: False

815. **The Chinese New Year begins on 1 January.**
a: True b: False

816. **The smallest country in the world is called Vatican City. It's inhabited by...**
a: Between 5 and 10 people
b: Between 50 and 100 people
c: Between 500 and 1,000 people
d: Between 5,000 and 10,000 people

817. **Nomads are...**
a: People who move from place to place
b: People that live in the city of Noman
c: Juicy fruits that grow in the desert
d: A small animal found only in South Africa

818. **The country of Russia is spread across two continents.**
a: True b: False

819. **The biggest pyramid is the size of six football fields side by side.**
a: True b: False

820. **A place in the desert where water bubbles up is called an...**
a: Oase b: Oasu
c: Oaso d: Oasis

World travellers

821. What is a baby deer called?
a: A fawn b: A lamb
c: A piglet d: A calf

822. Which kind of animal likes to remove insects from the backs of buffaloes?
a: Monkeys b: Spiders
c: Birds d: Giraffes

823. Giant pandas have an extra thumb on their forepaws.
a: True b: False

824. Chimpanzees sleep on the ground.
a: True b: False

825. What colour is the white rhinoceros?
a: White b: Grey
c: Brown d: Black

826. The dominant male gorilla in a group is a...
a: Goldback
b: Bronzeback
c: Copperback
d: Silverback

827. Lionesses are allowed to eat first in lion families.
a: True b: False

828. Male deer have antlers.
a: True b: False

829. How many stomachs does a cow have?
a: 1 b: 2
c: 3 d: 4

830. What is another name for a baby koala?
a: Joey b: John
c: James d: Jacob

Brain challenge **831**

What do we call the place where a rabbit sleeps?

A warren

Wild animals

832. Which fingernail grows the fastest?
a: The nail on your little finger
b: The nail on your ring finger
c: The nail on your middle finger
d: The nail on your index finger

833. What do we call the smallest bone in the body?
a: The hammer **b:** The stirrup
c: The anvil **d:** The funny bone

834. The biggest bone in the body is in the upper leg.
a: True **b:** False

835. Head hair grows faster than beard hair.
a: True **b:** False

836. In which country do the world's tallest people (on average) live?
a: China **b:** Australia
c: Argentina **d:** The Netherlands

837. What is the hardest material in the body?
a: Dental enamel **b:** Bone
c: Muscles **d:** Nails

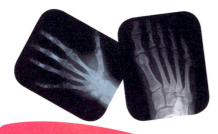

842 Brain challenge

How many teeth does an adult have?

32

838. Half of all the bones in your body are in your hands and feet.
a: True **b:** False

839. The smallest people in the world are called Pygmies.
a: True **b:** False

840. Which is the widest blood vessel in the body?
a: The capillary **b:** The forta
c: The aorta **d:** The venule

841. The most active muscles in your body are:
a: The muscles in your feet
b: The muscles in your hands
c: Your stomach muscles
d: Your eye muscles

Biology

853 *Brain challenge*

What kind of fruit is an Elstar?

An apple

---

847. How are cacti able to survive in arid regions?
a: They never need any water **b:** They store rainwater, which they later use in arid conditions **c:** They can't. Cacti die when subjected to arid conditions
d: Cacti don't grow in arid areas

848. There is more saltwater than freshwater on Earth.
a: True **b:** False

849. Cold climates are best for growing pineapples.
a: True **b:** False

850. Which material doesn't occur in nature?
a: Gold **b:** Rubber **c:** Plastic **d:** Wood

851. What shape are the fruit of the beech tree?
a: Triangular **b:** Star shaped
c: Circular **d:** Right angled

852. Flora means plants.
a: True **b:** False

---

843. Which plant doesn't sting or prick?
a: Thistles
b: Roses
c: Nettles
d: Violets

844. Polyester is a plant.
a: True **b:** False

845. Peanuts grow underground.
a: True **b:** False

846. Which tree stays green in the winter?
a: Oak
b: Beech
c: Pine
d: Sycamore

Nature

864 Brain challenge

Which animals are you afraid of if you suffer from arachnophobia?

Spiders

854. A spider is an insect.
a: True b: False

855. Butterflies have antennae.
a: True b: False

856. How many legs does an insect have?
a: 2 b: 4 c: 6 d: 8

857. What kind of animal is a firefly?
a: A fly b: A mosquito
c: A worm d: A beetle

858. Both female mosquitoes and male mosquitoes sting.
a: True b: False

859. Another name for a ladybird is a ladybug.
a: True b: False

860. Who lays the eggs in a bee colony?
a: Only the females
b: Only the males
c: Only the one-year-old bees
d: Only the queen

861. What is a new-born grasshopper called?
a: An elf
b: A nymph
c: A dwarf
d: A grasshopper chick

862. Female stick insects can only lay eggs if there is a male present.
a: True b: False

863. A caterpillar is a baby butterfly.
a: True b: False

Small creatures

854: b, 855: a, 856: c, 857: d, 858: b, 859: a, 860: d, 861: b, 862: b, 863: a

865. **What is Svalbard?**
a: A large waterfall in South Africa
b: An archipelago in Norway
c: A group of tall, pointed mountains in Russia
d: A volcano in New Zealand

866. **Which country is not in Europe?**
a: Spain b: Greece
c: Nepal d: Norway

867. **The North Pole is also called Antarctica.**
a: True b: False

868. **How many oceans are there on Earth?**
a: 7 b: 6
c: 5 d: 4

869. **Which city is also known as the 'City of Light'?**
a: New York b: Paris
c: Niger d: Lima

870. **What is the largest island in South America called?**
a: Greenland
b: Iceland
c: Fire Land
d: Easter Island

871. **Llanfairpwllgwyngyllgogerychwyrndrob-wllllantysiliogogogoch is a place in Wales.**
a: True b: False

872. **Uganda is a country in South America.**
a: True b: False

873. **Which shape features on the Danish, Swedish, Finnish and Norwegian flags?**
a: A star b: A circle
c: A cross d: A hexagon

874. **The outermost layer of the Earth is called the Earth's crust.**
a: True b: False

The Earth

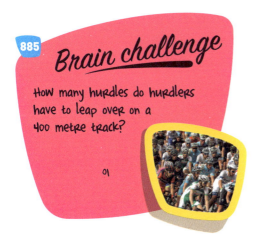

Brain challenge

How many hurdles do hurdlers have to leap over on a 400 metre track?

01

875. What is a group of cyclists called in a race?
a: A pack
b: A peloton
c: A parade
d: A herd

876. What is 'dribbling' in basketball?
a: When you trip over an opponent's leg
b: When you bounce the ball while running
c: When you catch the ball while jumping
d: When you throw the ball while falling

877. The word 'karateka' refers to someone who practices karate.
a: True b: False

878. The sticks used in golf are called 'canes'.
a: True b: False

879. Which sport involves dancing on 'pointe shoes'?
a: Street dancing b: Break dancing
c: Ballroom dancing d: Ballet

880. A fencer's protective clothing is usually:
a: Green b: Red
c: White d: Black

881. Water polo is a type of netball played in the water.
a: True b: False

882. Squash is always played outdoors.
a: True b: False

883. In which types of sport do you serve?
a: Cycling and autocross b: Sailing and surfing c: Tennis and volleyball d: Skating and skiing

884. In platform diving, two swimmers make exactly the same movements in the water.
a: True b: False

Sport

886. Red wood ants prefer to make their nest...
a: Under the ground, in the sand
b: Above the ground, with pine needles
c: In the top of a tree
d: None of the above: they don't have nests

887. How many eyes does a grasshopper have?
a: 1 b: 2
c: 5 d: 10

888. Mosquitoes lay eggs.
a: True b: False

889. You can tell how old a ladybird is by counting the spots on its back.
a: True b: False

890. What is the creature that is like a snail without a shell called?
a: A naked slug
b: A bare slug
c: A semi-slug
d: A slug

891. What colour is the blood of many insects?
a: Red-orange
b: Grey-black
c: Yellow-green
d: Blue-green

892. A stag beetle is an insect.
a: True b: False

893. Fireflies produce light to find a partner.
a: True b: False

894. How many wings does a dragonfly have?
a: 2 b: 4 c: 6 d: 8

895. Cockroaches look like:
a: Frogs b: Beetles
c: Spiders d: Mosquitoes

Small creatures

896. What are the Galápagos Islands known for?
a: No humans have ever been on the islands
b: They are inhabited by animals found nowhere else in the world
c: They are imaginary islands, but many people think they really exist
d: They are the world's smallest islands

897. The red dot on the Japanese flag represents the sun.
a: True **b:** False

898. Where will you find man-made islands shaped like palm trees?
a: Off the coast of Spain
b: Off the coast of the United States
c: Off the coast of Dubai
d: Off the coast of India

899. What does the white dot on the flag of Laos represent?
a: The Sun **b:** The Moon
c: A star **d:** The Earth

900. Greenland is a very green country with many forests.
a: True **b:** False

901. Many markets float on water in South-East Asia.
a: True **b:** False

902. Australians celebrate the New Year in the...
a: Spring **b:** Summer
c: Winter **d:** Autumn

903. The earliest inhabitants of America are called Native Americans.
a: True **b:** False

904. Which queen do you see most often on banknotes across the world?
a: The Queen of Norway
b: The Queen of Sweden
c: The Queen of Jordan
d: The Queen of England

905. The most common surname in the world is 'Smith'.
a: True **b:** False

906 Brain challenge

What is the capital of Iraq?

Baghdad

World travellers

907. Palaeontologists study fossilised animals and plants.
a: True b: False

908. Mammoths were a type of bird.
a: True b: False

909. What does the word 'dinosaur' mean?
a: Big predator
b: Strong reptile
c: Terrible lizard
d: Extra-terrestrial being

910. The extinct Irish elk or 'Megaloceros giganteus' was given its Latin name because...
a: It was the biggest elk that ever lived on Earth
b: Its antlers were enormous
c: It could make an awful lot of noise
d: It was the strongest animal of its time

911. Why do animals sometimes die out?
a: Because the climate changes
b: Because the living environment changes
c: Because people hunt animals
d: All of the above

912. Tortoises could fly in the time of the dinosaurs.
a: True b: False

913. Which animal species is not threatened with extinction?
a: Giant panda b: Orang-utan
c: Hyena d: Rhinoceros

914. Rhinoceroses are hunted because people want to make drugs from...
a: Their horns b: Their skin
c: Their tail d: Their legs

915. All dinosaurs were huge.
a: True b: False

916. The Triceratops dinosaur had five horns on his head.
a: True b: False

Extinct and threatend animals

917. How far is the Earth from the Sun?
a: 149 kilometres
b: 149 thousand kilometres
c: 149 million kilometres
d: 149 billion kilometres

918. The Earth turns on its axis around 500 metres a second.
a: True b: False

919. Ebb and flow are caused by the Moon's gravitational pull.
a: True b: False

920. What is another word for whirlwind?
a: Tornado b: Avalanche
c: Hurricane d: Thunderstorm

921. Sometimes the ocean's waves are taller than a 10-storey apartment block.
a: True b: False

922. A leap year is one day longer than a 'normal' year.
a: True b: False

923. How often do leap years occur?
a: Once every two years
b: Once every four years
c: Once every eight years
d: Once every twelve years

924. What does a meteorologist study?
a: The stars b: The volcanoes
c: The oceans d: The weather

925. You can draw with charcoal.
a: True b: False

926. How deep is the deepest point in the Earth's oceans?
a: Around 11 metres
b: Around 100 metres
c: Around 1 kilometre
d: Around 11 kilometres

927 *Brain challenge*

In which season is January in Australia?

Summer

The Earth

928. Pharaoh is another word for a king of ancient Egypt.
a: True b: False

929. The word 'knight' is from medieval times and means...
a: Horse rider b: Harness wearer
c: Hooligan d: Strong man

930. How many paintings did Vincent van Gogh sell during this lifetime?
a: 0 b: 1 c: 100 d: 1 million

931. The shields that Roman soldiers once carried were roughly as big as...
a: A hand b: A leg
c: A chair d: A door

932. What nationality was the first person to bring a potato to Europe?
a: Dutch b: Spanish
c: French d: Belgian

933. The days of the week are named after Greek flowers.
a: True b: False

934. Who discovered that the world is round and not flat?
a: Abel Tasman b: Marco Polo
c: Columbus d: The ancient Greeks

935. A list of events in chronological order begins with the events that happened last.
a: True b: False

936. What does the Roman numeral X mean?
a: 1 b: 2 c: 5 d: 10

937. When Columbus discovered America, he actually thought he'd arrived in India.
a: True b: False

World travellers

938. Which sport is 'Formula 1'?
a: Auto racing **b:** Cycle racing
c: Motorbike racing **d:** Boat racing

939. In kite surfing, a surfer is pulled across the water by a kite.
a: True **b:** False

940. Who performs the still rings in gymnastics at the Olympic Games?
a: Only men
b: Only women
c: Men and women
d: No one – this event isn't performed at the Olympic Games

941. What is the name of the disc that hockey players try to score with?
a: Duck **b:** Tuck **c:** Puck **d:** Muck

942. The long jump world record of 8.95 metres was set in 1991.
a: True **b:** False

943. The triathlon consists of swimming, cycling and golf.
a: True **b:** False

944. What does the Japanese word judo mean?
a: Gentle fall
b: Hard throw
c: Gentle way
d: Hard mat

945. Which sport is sometimes played underwater?
a: Hockey **b:** Football
c: Rugby **d:** All of the above

946. Bodybuilding is only practiced by men.
a: True **b:** False

947. The 'pancake' is a type of dive in volleyball.
a: True **b:** False

Sport

948. You have 10 bags. Each bag contains 3 apples. You have 30 apples in total.
a: True **b:** False

949. All the sides of a square are the same length.
a: True **b:** False

950. It is 10 o'clock in the morning. What time will it be in three-quarters of an hour?
a: Quarter past 10
b: Half past 10
c: Quarter to 11
d: 11 o'clock

951. A 500 gram golden nugget weighs more than a 500 gram cushion.
a: True **b:** False

952. Which sum produces the answer 12?
a: 4 + 3 **b:** 10 + 3 **c:** 16 − 8 **d:** 8 + 4

953. How many grams does a 35 kilo child weigh?
a: 350 **b:** 3,500
c: 35,000 **d:** 350,000

954. There are 30 minutes in half an hour.
a: True **b:** False

955. 6 children are each wearing 2 socks, which means they are wearing 10 socks altogether.
a: True **b:** False

956. 60 children are going on a school trip. A bus seats 20 children. How many buses are needed?
a: 1 **b:** 2 **c:** 3 **d:** 4

957. Which number is uneven?
a: 2 **b:** 4 **c:** 7 **d:** 10

Mathematics

968 Brain challenge

What is the largest city in China?

Shanghai.

958. The Dead Sea is around 400 metres below sea level.
a: True **b:** False

959. What is the highest weather temperature ever to have been recorded on Earth?
a: Almost 48 degrees Celsius
b: Almost 58 degrees Celsius
c: Almost 68 degrees Celsius
d: Almost 78 degrees Celsius

960. If you were to tie a rope around the earth, how long would it have to be?
a: 400 km **b:** 4,000 km
c: 40,000 km **d:** 400,000 km

961. Coal is formed from the remains of plants that have been buried deep in the Earth for a very long time.
a: True **b:** False

962. An uncut diamond is worth more than a cut diamond.
a: True **b:** False

963. What did New York used to be called?
a: New Amsterdam **b:** New Brussels
c: New London **d:** New Town

964. What do Japanese people call their country?
a: Japan **b:** Nippon **c:** Tokyo **d:** Gohan

965. Almost a third of all land on Earth is desert.
a: True **b:** False

966. How many days are there in a year?
a: 120 **b:** 248 **c:** 365 **d:** 498

967. Canberra is the capital of Australia.
a: True **b:** False

The Earth

Brain challenge

979

What is the world's second-largest mountain?

969. What is another word for Viking?
a: Norseman **b:** Fjord raider
c: Celt **d:** Knarr

970. How long did it take the Chinese to build the Great Wall?
a: 2 years **b:** 20 years
c: 200 years **d:** 2,000 years

971. Samurai were warriors from China.
a: True **b:** False

972. What do we call a period of 100 years?
a: A decade
b: A century
c: A millennium
d: An anniversary

973. Which language were most books written in throughout the Middle Ages?
a: Greek **b:** Latin
c: English **d:** Spanish

974. The ancient Egyptians thought that crocodiles flooded the River Nile.
a: True **b:** False

975. What does the Roman numeral V mean?
a: 1 **b:** 2
c: 5 **d:** 10

976. Most countries write their numbers as 1, 2, 3, etc. In which country does this writing style originate?
a: Russia
b: China
c: India
d: England

977. Leonardo da Vinci was an Italian painter and inventor.
a: True **b:** False

978. Some months are named after Roman emperors and gods.
a: True **b:** False

World travellers

969: a 970: d 971: b 972: b 973: b 974: a 975: c 976: c 977: a 978: a

Brain challenge

What do we call animals that only eat plant material?

Herbivores

980. Which type of present-day animal is descended from the dinosaurs?
a: Birds **b:** Mammals
c: Lizards **d:** Insects

981. Today's tigers descend from the sabre-toothed cat.
a: True **b:** False

982. Dinosaurs were mammals.
a: True **b:** False

983. When did the dinosaurs go extinct?
a: 65 years ago
b: 6500 years ago
c: 65,000 years ago
d: 65 million years ago

984. Polar bears live...
a: On the North Pole
b: On the South Pole
c: On the North and South Poles
d: On neither of the Poles

985. A blue whale's tongue weighs as much as an African elephant.
a: True **b:** False

986. The dodo could fly well.
a: True **b:** False

987. The heaviest dinosaur weighed as much as:
a: 1 elephant **b:** 10 elephants
c: 25 elephants **d:** 50 elephants

988. The extinct sabre-toothed cat had very long, canine teeth.
a: True **b:** False

989. Tigers can't swim.
a: True **b:** False

Extinct and threatend animals

991. In the form of which letter do geese fly?
a: The letter S b: The letter T
c: The letter U d: The letter V

992. If a guinea fowl is frightened, it...
a: Runs away
b: Freezes on the spot
c: Begins to screech
d: Becomes very quiet

993. Doves never get lost.
a: True b: False

994. The elf owl is the smallest owl in the world.
a: True b: False

995. What do we call the noise that geese make?
a: Quacking b: Honking
c: Laughing d: Giggling

996. Birds sometimes travel to warmer climes at the end of the summer. What do we call this?
a: Bird travel b: Bird holiday
c: Bird migration d: Bird flight

997. Swans search for a new partner every year.
a: True b: False

998. Parakeets usually sleep on one leg.
a: True b: False

999. Woodpeckers 'talk' with one another...
a: By whistling
b: By drumming
c: By flapping their wings
d: By turning their heads

1000. Chickens clean their feathers...
a: In a bath of water
b: In a bath of lather
c: In a bath of mud
d: In a bath of dust

Birds